posh®
Coloring
BOOK

· · · · · · · · · · · · · · · · · · ·

INSPIRED GARDEN
SOOTHING DESIGNS
FOR FUN & RELAXATION

Susan Black

· · · · · · · · · · · · · · · · · · ·

Andrews McMeel
Publishing®
a division of Andrews McMeel Universal

POSH® COLORING BOOK
INSPIRED GARDEN
SOOTHING DESIGNS FOR FUN & RELAXATION

Andrews McMeel Publishing
a division of Andrews McMeel Universal
1130 Walnut Street, Kansas City, Missouri 64106

www.andrewsmcmeel.com

16 17 18 19 20 MLY 10 9 8 7 6 5 4 3 2 1

ISBN: 978-1-4494-7836-0

ATTENTION: SCHOOLS AND BUSINESSES
Andrews McMeel books are available at quantity discounts with bulk purchase for educational, business, or sales promotional use. For information, please e-mail the Andrews McMeel Publishing Special Sales Department: specialsales@amuniversal.com.

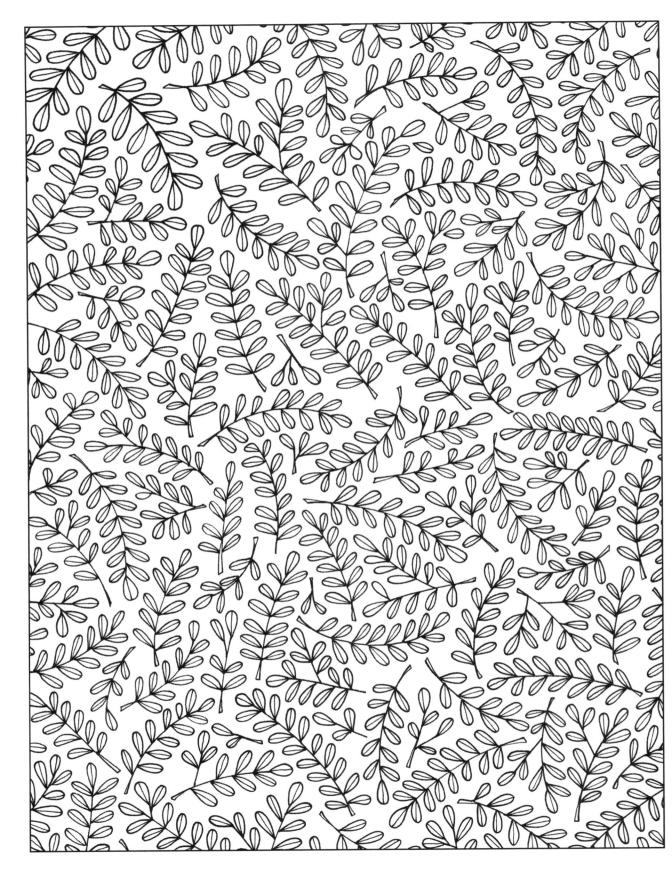

EVERY breath is a new BEGINNING